Cyber Security and IoT - The Future

Mark Hayward

Published by Mark Hayward, 2025.

Table of Contents

Title Page

Cyber Security and IoT - The Future

Table of Contents

1. Introduction to IoT and Cyber Security

2. Risks and Threats in IoT Environments

3. Security Protocols for IoT

4. Device Authentication and Identity Management

5. Network Security for IoT

6. Data Privacy and Protection in IoT

7. Incident Response and Management in IoT

8. The Role of AI and Machine Learning in IoT Security

9. Future Trends in IoT and Cyber Security

10. Best Practices for IoT Security

11. Regulatory Compliance and Standards for IoT Security

12. Building a Cyber Security Culture for IoT

13. Collaboration and Information Sharing in IoT Security

14. Challenges and Barriers to IoT Security

15. Conclusion: The Road Ahead for IoT and Cyber Security

Cyber Security and IoT - The Future

About

With over 23 years of experience in cyber security, this author is a distinguished veteran of the UK Armed Forces who has honed their expertise while serving in both independent and prominent organizational roles. Their commitment to providing exceptional cyber security services to local and central government departments reflects a deep understanding of safeguarding digital landscapes. This unique blend of military discipline and industry know-how allows them to make complex concepts accessible and engaging, establishing their voice as a formidable authority in the evolving realm of cyber security and IoT.

Table of Contents

1. Introduction to IoT and Cyber Security

(1) - 1.1 Understanding IoT: Definition and Components
    (2) - 1.2 The Relationship Between IoT and Cyber Security
    (3) - 1.3 Current Trends in IoT Cyber Security

2. Risks and Threats in IoT Environments

(1) - 2.1 Common IoT Vulnerabilities
    (2) - 2.2 Threat Models for IoT Devices
    (3) - 2.3 Case Studies of IoT Attacks

3. Security Protocols for IoT

(1) - 3.1 Overview of IoT Security Protocols
    (2) - 3.2 Analyzing Encryption Techniques for IoT
    (3) - 3.3 Access Control Mechanisms in IoT

4. Device Authentication and Identity Management

(1) - 4.1 Authentication Methods in IoT
    (2) - 4.2 Identity Management Challenges in IoT
    (3) - 4.3 Best Practices for Device Authentication

5. Network Security for IoT

(1) - 5.1 Secure Network Architecture for IoT
    (2) - 5.2 Intrusion Detection Systems in IoT Networks
    (3) - 5.3 Role of Firewalls in IoT Security

6. Data Privacy and Protection in IoT

(1) - 6.1 Challenges to Data Privacy in IoT
    (2) - 6.2 Legal and Regulatory Considerations
    (3) - 6.3 Effective Data Protection Strategies

7. Incident Response and Management in IoT

(1) - 7.1 Developing an Incident Response Plan for IoT
    (2) - 7.2 Forensics in IoT Security Breaches
    (3) - 7.3 Learning from IoT Security Incidents

8. The Role of AI and Machine Learning in IoT Security

(1) - 8.1 Leveraging AI for Threat Detection
    (2) - 8.2 Machine Learning Techniques for IoT Security
    (3) - 8.3 Ethical Considerations in AI-Driven Security

9. Future Trends in IoT and Cyber Security

(1) - 9.1 Evolution of IoT Architecture
    (2) - 9.2 Predicting Future Security Challenges
    (3) - 9.3 Emerging Technologies Impacting IoT Security

10. Best Practices for IoT Security

(1) - 10.1 Security by Design Principles
    (2) - 10.2 Developing Secure Applications for IoT
    (3) - 10.3 Continuous Monitoring and Improvement

11. Regulatory Compliance and Standards for IoT Security

(1) - 11.1 Overview of IoT Security Standards
    (2) - 11.2 Compliance Challenges and Solutions
    (3) - 11.3 Best Practices for Achieving Compliance

12. Building a Cyber Security Culture for IoT

(1) - 12.1 Employee Training and Awareness
    (2) - 12.2 Creating Policies for IoT Security
    (3) - 12.3 Fostering a Security Mindset in Organizations

13. Collaboration and Information Sharing in IoT Security

(1) - 13.1 Importance of Collaboration Among Stakeholders
    (2) - 13.2 Platforms for Information Sharing
    (3) - 13.3 Building Trust in Information Sharing Networks

14. Challenges and Barriers to IoT Security

(1) - 14.1 Technical Challenges in Securing IoT
    (2) - 14.2 Economic and Resource Constraints
    (3) - 14.3 Cultural Barriers to Security Implementation

15. Conclusion: The Road Ahead for IoT and Cyber Security

(1) - 15.1 Summary of Key Takeaways
    (2) - 15.2 Strategic Recommendations for Cyber Security Professionals
    (3) - 15.3 Preparing for the Future of IoT Security

1. Introduction to IoT and Cyber Security

1.1 Understanding IoT: Definition and Components

The Internet of Things, or IoT, refers to the network of interconnected devices that communicate and exchange data with one another over the internet. This ecosystem comprises various components that together establish a seamless flow of information. The primary components of IoT include devices such as sensors, actuators, and smart appliances, all of which collect and transmit data. Networks function as the backbone of IoT, providing the necessary infrastructure for these devices to communicate effectively. Various protocols, including Wi-Fi, Bluetooth, and cellular communication, play a critical role in ensuring that data can be sent and received efficiently. The applications of IoT are vast, ranging from smart homes that automate everyday tasks to complex industrial systems that monitor and optimize processes in real-time. Understanding these components is essential for anyone seeking to grasp the operational potential and security implications of IoT systems.

Connectivity is the lifeblood of IoT, enabling devices to interact and collaborate to enhance operational efficiencies across multiple sectors. In industries such as manufacturing, connectivity allows for real-time data collection and analysis, leading to predictive maintenance and reduced downtime. In healthcare, connected devices facilitate remote patient monitoring, allowing for timely interventions and improved patient outcomes. The retail sector benefits from IoT connectivity through inventory management systems that track stock levels and consumer preferences in real time, optimizing supply chains and enhancing customer experiences. Moreover, in smart cities, interconnected systems enable better resource management, traffic flow optimization, and energy conservation, all of which contribute to improved quality of life. The significance of connectivity cannot be overstated; it transforms traditional processes and drives innovation while presenting unique challenges, especially from a cybersecurity perspective.

For cybersecurity professionals, keeping pace with the rapidly evolving landscape of IoT is crucial not only for safeguarding networks but also for enhancing the overall security posture of organizations. As devices proliferate and become increasingly sophisticated, so do the potential vulnerabilities associated with their connectivity. Each point of connection can serve as an entry point for cyber threats, making it imperative to implement robust security measures. Practicing vigilant monitoring and proactive incident response strategies, along with adopting a comprehensive security framework tailored for IoT environments, will be key to mitigating risks. Staying informed about industry standards and best practices can significantly bolster the effectiveness of security protocols in protecting against malicious attacks.

1.2 The Relationship Between IoT and Cyber Security

The rapid proliferation of Internet of Things (IoT) devices has introduced a range of unique security vulnerabilities that cybersecurity professionals must navigate. Each device, from smart thermostats to industrial sensors, often has its own set of security protocols, or more frequently, lacks sufficient security measures altogether. Many of these devices collect and transmit sensitive data across networks without adequate encryption, leaving them susceptible to interception and unauthorized access. Moreover, the sheer number of connected devices has increased the attack surface for potential threats. Cybercriminals can exploit poorly secured devices to penetrate networks, disrupt services, or even create botnets. This vulnerability is exacerbated by the tendency of users to overlook security updates or use default credentials, which can render even the most advanced systems open to exploitation. As IoT devices continue to become integral in both personal and industrial contexts, understanding these vulnerabilities is critical for effective risk management and security planning.

The interconnected nature of IoT systems significantly heightens the importance of security measures. When devices are linked, a security breach in one can lead to a cascade of failures, resulting in extensive damage to the entire network. This interconnectedness requires cybersecurity strategies that account for the entire ecosystem of devices, rather than isolating security to individual components. Cybersecurity professionals must adopt a holistic approach toward securing IoT networks, which includes implementing end-to-end encryption, frequent vulnerability assessments, and robust monitoring systems. Additionally, educating users about secure practices—such as regularly changing passwords and ensuring their devices are updated—can vastly improve the defense against potential threats. As the technical landscape continues to evolve, prioritizing security in the design and implementation of IoT devices will not only protect data but also enhance the overall integrity and reliability of connected systems.

One practical tip for cybersecurity professionals is to encourage collaboration among manufacturers, developers, and users to establish standardized security protocols for IoT devices. By advocating for best practices and regulatory frameworks, the industry can move towards a more secure environment, ensuring that all stakeholders are aligned on the importance of maintaining robust cybersecurity measures in the face of an ever-expanding digital landscape.

1.3 Current Trends in IoT Cyber Security

Recent developments in IoT security practices have shifted the landscape significantly for device manufacturers. Increasing awareness of cyber threats has pressured these manufacturers to adopt stricter security measures throughout the product lifecycle. One consequential trend is the implementation of security by design principles, where security features are integrated from the earliest design phases, rather than being retrofitted after the fact. This proactive approach not only mitigates risks but also enhances consumer trust, which is critical in a market rife with scrutiny over data integrity and privacy. Additionally, manufacturers are beginning to adhere to regulatory compliance frameworks that mandate robust security controls. This is particularly relevant in sectors like healthcare and automotive, where IoT devices play a crucial role, and a breach could have dire consequences. Security practices such as regular firmware updates, vulnerability assessments, and risk management protocols are now seen as non-negotiable components of product development.

Emerging technologies and strategies are continually shaping the landscape of IoT cyber security. Artificial intelligence is making strides in threat detection, using machine learning algorithms to analyze massive amounts of data and identify anomalous behaviour that may indicate a breach. This capability allows companies to respond to threats in real time, reducing response times and minimizing potential damage. Moreover, the rise of blockchain technology offers a promising solution for ensuring device authentication and data integrity, as its decentralized nature makes it difficult for malicious actors to tamper with data exchanges between IoT devices. Another strategy gaining traction is the concept of Zero Trust architecture, which assumes that threats could be both external and internal. This mindset emphasizes continuous verification of device identities and requires robust authentication measures, even for devices within the network perimeter. As the number of connected devices skyrockets, the collaboration between cybersecurity professionals and IoT developers will be crucial to implement comprehensive security measures that can evolve with emerging threats.

A practical consideration for cybersecurity professionals is the importance of embedding security training into the culture of IoT development teams. This not only enhances knowledge about current threats but also fosters a security-first mentality that permeates all levels of product design and deployment. Investing in ongoing education and utilizing frameworks that outline best practices can significantly elevate the security posture of IoT devices, ultimately contributing to a safer interconnected future.

2. Risks and Threats in IoT Environments

2.1 Common IoT Vulnerabilities

Prevalent security flaws in Internet of Things (IoT) devices often stem from fundamental oversights during the design and deployment processes. One of the most significant vulnerabilities is the use of default credentials. Many manufacturers ship devices with preset usernames and passwords that are well-known or easily guessable. When users neglect to change these credentials, it creates a significant entry point for attackers. Additionally, insufficient encryption plays a critical role in the security landscape. Many IoT devices transmit data over the internet without adequate protection, leaving sensitive information vulnerable to interception. This lack of encryption means that data can be easily captured and exploited, which is particularly concerning for devices that handle personal information or control critical infrastructure.

The consequences of these vulnerabilities can be dire. Malicious actors can exploit default credentials to gain unauthorized access to devices, leading to potential network intrusions and the manipulation of functionalities. For instance, an attacker could turn a home security camera into a surveillance tool to spy on users or access a smart thermostat to control heating and cooling, leading to energy waste or increased utility costs. Insufficient encryption allows hackers to perform man-in-the-middle attacks, where they intercept data being transmitted between the device and its server. This not only facilitates data theft but also raises the risk of deploying malware into the system, further compromising security and integrity. Such breaches can have lasting ramifications, not only for individual users but also for organizations that rely on IoT devices for operational efficiency.

Understanding these vulnerabilities is crucial for cyber security professionals who must anticipate and mitigate risks associated with IoT connectivity. Regular audits of IoT devices, combined with strict adherence to security best practices like changing default credentials and implementing robust encryption protocols, are essential strategies. It is also beneficial to ensure that devices are regularly updated with the latest firmware, which can address known security flaws. Additionally, integrating network monitoring tools to detect unusual activity can provide another layer of defense against potential attacks. Employing these proactive measures can significantly reduce the threat landscape of IoT environments.

2.2 Threat Models for IoT Devices

Developing a comprehensive framework for understanding potential threat vectors against IoT devices involves identifying and analyzing various attack surfaces that could be exploited by malicious actors. IoT devices often operate with minimal security features, making them attractive targets. These devices may connect to the internet directly or through gateways, which serve as entry points for attackers. Understanding these avenues of intrusion helps in mapping out potential vulnerabilities, such as weak default passwords, unpatched firmware, and inadequate encryption practices. The threat landscape is further complicated by the integration of IoT devices within larger networks, which may expose them to broader attacks, such as Distributed Denial of Service (DDoS) attacks or exploitation of poorly configured network settings. Additionally, threats can stem from a variety of actors, ranging from script kiddies to organized cybercrime groups, and each has different motivations and techniques that they may employ against IoT systems.

The impact of these threats on the confidentiality, integrity, and availability of data is significant and must not be underestimated. Compromised IoT devices can lead to unauthorized access to sensitive information, threatening confidentiality. For instance, if an IoT camera is hacked, the intruder might gain access to live feeds, potentially violating privacy policies and personal privacy. Integrity is also at risk, as IoT devices could be manipulated to send false data, which can disrupt the functioning of critical applications, such as healthcare devices or industrial controls, leading to potentially life-threatening situations. Availability can be compromised through various means, especially via ransomware attacks that can render devices inoperative until a ransom is paid. The interconnected nature of IoT systems means that the cascading consequences of a single compromised device can extend far beyond its immediate application, impacting entire networks and the services they provide.

To navigate this evolving landscape successfully, cybersecurity professionals must prioritize a multi-layered security strategy that includes robust authentication measures, regular firmware updates, and continuous monitoring of device activity. Establishing clear incident response protocols is also crucial, enabling teams to act swiftly in the event of a breach. Additionally, training users on best practices for IoT device management, such as changing default passwords and recognizing phishing attempts, can enhance overall security posture. Understanding and mitigating the potential threats to IoT devices is an ongoing challenge that requires vigilance and proactive measures.

2.3 Case Studies of IoT Attacks

Real-world examples of IoT security breaches illustrate the vulnerabilities present in connected devices. One notable incident occurred in 2016 when the Mirai botnet exploited unsecured IoT devices to launch a massive DDoS attack on Dyn, a major DNS provider. This attack disrupted access to prominent websites like Netflix, Twitter, and Airbnb, showcasing how weak security practices surrounding IoT can lead to widespread chaos. The attack's aftermath emphasized the need for improved security protocols, as many devices were easily compromised due to default passwords and insufficient protections.

Another significant case was the 2020 attack on a water treatment facility in Oldsmar, Florida. Hackers gained access to the facility's SCADA system through an insecure remote access point, tampering with the chemical levels meant to treat the water supply. Fortunately, operators noticed the unusual changes before any damage could be done. This incident highlighted the critical nature of securing not just consumer devices but also industrial IoT systems that can have far-reaching implications on public safety. The consequences of such breaches can range from economic losses to severe safety hazards, underlining the urgency for robust security measures.

The lessons learned from these incidents serve as a vital guide for future security practices. One key takeaway is the necessity of adopting a security-first mindset in the design and deployment of IoT devices, ensuring best practices like regular firmware updates, multifactor authentication, and rigorous access controls. Additionally, organizations need to conduct regular assessments of their IoT ecosystem to identify and rectify vulnerabilities proactively. By implementing comprehensive security strategies tailored to the unique challenges posed by IoT devices, cybersecurity professionals can significantly mitigate risks associated with these technologies. Maintaining an awareness of emerging threats and adapting security policies accordingly will lead to a stronger overall defense against potential attacks.

3. Security Protocols for IoT

3.1 Overview of IoT Security Protocols

Various security protocols are essential for protecting IoT systems from threats and vulnerabilities. These protocols govern how devices communicate and exchange data, ensuring that sensitive information remains safe from unauthorized access. Protocols such as Transport Layer Security (TLS) and Internet Protocol Security (IPsec) play a crucial role in encrypting data transmitted between devices. Lightweight protocols like Datagram Transport Layer Security (DTLS) are tailored for resource-constrained environments typical in IoT, providing a secure transport layer without overwhelming the devices' limited processing capabilities. Additionally, protocols like the Constrained Application Protocol (CoAP) are specifically designed for low-bandwidth links and often incorporate built-in security mechanisms to enhance the integrity and confidentiality of messages exchanged in an IoT environment.

These protocols safeguard communication and data within IoT frameworks by implementing encryption, authentication, and integrity checks. Encryption ensures that any intercepted data cannot be easily read or manipulated by attackers, while authentication verifies the identities of the communicating devices, preventing impersonation. As data flows through an IoT network, integrity checks help ensure that messages have not been tampered with during transmission. For example, protocols like MQTT can be secured using TLS to ensure that messages sent between IoT devices are both confidential and authentic. Implementing these measures creates a multi-layered defense strategy that significantly reduces the risk of data breaches and other security incidents in the expanding landscape of IoT technologies.

Staying informed about the latest developments in IoT security protocols can greatly enhance the security posture of any organization. Cybersecurity professionals should regularly review and update their security practices, considering new threats and vulnerabilities as they emerge. Greater awareness of protocol specifications and their potential weaknesses will empower professionals to make informed decisions when integrating IoT devices into existing networks, helping maintain robust security in an increasingly interconnected world.

3.2 Analyzing Encryption Techniques for IoT

Investigating different encryption methodologies suitable for protecting IoT communications requires a deep understanding of the unique challenges these devices face. Traditional encryption methods, such as symmetric and asymmetric cryptography, have their merits but must be adapted for the constraints of IoT devices, which often operate with limited processing power and memory. Lightweight encryption algorithms, such as Advanced Encryption Standard (AES) in a truncated version, and Elliptic Curve Cryptography (ECC) offer viable alternatives. AES provides strong security and can be implemented efficiently, while ECC allows for smaller key sizes, enhancing speed and reducing overhead. Further evaluation of other methods includes the use of hash functions for data integrity and authentication protocols that ensure secure device communication. Tailoring these methodologies to the specific requirements of IoT applications is essential to maintaining confidentiality and integrity during data transmission.

Evaluating the trade-offs between security strength and computational efficiency in IoT devices is crucial. Higher security often demands more computational resources, which can be a limiting factor for many IoT applications. For instance, while a method like RSA can provide robust security, its extensive key size and complex calculations can hinder performance on a resource-constrained device. Conversely, a lightweight encryption approach may sacrifice some degree of security to enhance efficiency. Cyber security professionals must strike an optimal balance when selecting encryption techniques, considering the sensitivity of the data, the environment in which the IoT device operates, and the potential threats it faces. By evaluating how various encryption methods can be integrated without overwhelming device capabilities, professionals can devise strategies that ensure both security and performance.

Understanding these principles is particularly important as IoT devices become more integrated into critical infrastructures. Ensuring that devices can communicate securely while maintaining performance efficiency allows for a resilient network that can withstand potential cyber threats. A practical approach involves implementing a layered security strategy that incorporates device-level encryption, secure communication protocols, and regular updates to address emerging vulnerabilities. By remaining vigilant and agile in adapting these encryption methodologies, professionals can effectively safeguard IoT environments and the networks they connect to.

3.3 Access Control Mechanisms in IoT

Access control in IoT is vital for ensuring the integrity and security of interconnected devices. Various models exist that regulate device authentication and user permissions. The Role-Based Access Control (RBAC) model, for example, grants access based on user roles, ensuring that only those with the appropriate permissions can interact with specific devices. Attribute-Based Access Control (ABAC) enhances this by taking into account user attributes and environmental conditions, allowing for dynamic access decisions. Another growing approach is the Policy-Based Access Control (PBAC), which allows organizations to define rules that dictate access based on more granular criteria. Each of these models plays a crucial role in mitigating risks associated with unauthorized access to IoT systems, tailoring access based on specific needs and user responsibilities.

The effectiveness of these access control models in preventing unauthorized access hinges on their implementation and adaptability. RBAC, while straightforward and easy to administer, may struggle in environments where users' roles frequently change. ABAC offers greater flexibility and granularity, but it requires a more complex setup and might introduce latency in decision-making. PBAC allows for comprehensive access policies but necessitates careful management to prevent the proliferation of overly complex rules that could lead to vulnerabilities. Ultimately, a robust evaluation of each model's strengths and weaknesses is essential. Organizations must also consider the evolving landscape of IoT technologies, where new devices join the network continuously, necessitating adaptive control mechanisms to secure sensitive data and maintain system integrity.

4. Device Authentication and Identity Management

4.1 Authentication Methods in IoT

Various authentication techniques are employed to verify the identity of IoT devices, ensuring that only trusted devices can connect to the network. One common approach is the use of symmetric key cryptography, where a shared secret key is utilized for authentication. This method is efficient but poses a risk, especially if the key is compromised, as it can grant unauthorized access to the network. Public key infrastructure (PKI) offers a more secure alternative by using asymmetric cryptography. In this setup, each device has a unique pair of public and private keys, allowing for secure identity verification and data encryption. X.509 certificates are often employed within this framework to authenticate devices and establish trust hierarchies. Additionally, lightweight cryptographic protocols, such as the Authentication and Key Agreement (AKA), are gaining traction, particularly for resource-constrained devices, enabling secure communication while minimizing overhead.

Managing identities in large-scale IoT deployments presents significant challenges. As the number of connected devices skyrockets, the complexity of maintaining a secure and efficient identity management system increases. One major issue is the sheer volume of devices, leading to a heightened attack surface that cyber criminals can exploit. Furthermore, the diversity of devices and operating systems complicates the implementation of standardized authentication protocols. This diversity can hinder interoperability, making it difficult for devices from different manufacturers to authenticate seamlessly. The dynamic nature of IoT networks, where devices frequently join and leave the network, adds another layer of challenge. Continuous monitoring and identity verification become essential to ensure that only legitimate devices remain connected. Resource limitations in some devices also restrict the implementation of sophisticated authentication mechanisms, making them vulnerable to attacks.

Understanding these challenges is critical for cybersecurity professionals as they design robust security frameworks for IoT ecosystems. Implementing automated identity management solutions could alleviate some of these burdens, enabling real-time monitoring and policy enforcement across various devices. Employing machine learning techniques may also help anticipate potential security threats by analyzing patterns in device behaviour. Ensuring firmware updates and patches for connected devices can further bolster defenses. By staying informed on the latest authentication strategies and potential pitfalls in large-scale deployments, cybersecurity professionals can enhance the security posture of IoT networks and mitigate risks effectively.

4.2 Identity Management Challenges in IoT

Maintaining accurate and secure identity management across diverse IoT devices presents several key challenges. One of the primary issues lies in the sheer scale and variety of devices that comprise the IoT ecosystem. With millions of devices, each with potentially different specifications and operating systems, it becomes increasingly difficult to implement a uniform identity management strategy. Additionally, many IoT devices have limited computing resources and lack advanced security features, making them vulnerable to unauthorized access. This vulnerability can lead to significant security breaches, where an attacker can exploit a compromised device to access sensitive networks and data.

Another challenge arises from the dynamic nature of IoT environments. Devices frequently connect and disconnect from networks, and this transient behaviour complicates the creation and enforcement of identity verification protocols. Furthermore, the storage and management of identity information must be carefully regulated to prevent data theft or loss. The distributed architecture of IoT networks can lead to a lack of visibility and control over device identities, making it difficult for security professionals to monitor and manage identities effectively.

To effectively address identity lifecycle management in IoT, organizations can adopt several potential solutions. Implementing a centralized identity management system can help streamline the onboarding and offboarding processes for devices. This system could leverage automated workflows to provision identities as devices connect and deprovision them when devices are retired or disconnected. Additionally, utilizing strong authentication methods, such as device certificates or biometrics, can significantly enhance security by ensuring that only authorized devices are granted access to the network.

Moreover, establishing a robust governance framework for identity management plays a crucial role. This framework should include regular audits and continuous monitoring of device identities to identify and remediate any anomalies promptly. Incorporating machine learning algorithms can also help predict unusual device behaviour, providing additional layers of security. Emphasizing user awareness and providing adequate training for cybersecurity professionals are key in recognizing the importance of maintaining identity integrity within IoT ecosystems.

Ultimately, investing time and resources in developing comprehensive identity management strategies for IoT can significantly mitigate risks associated with identity mismanagement. Encouraging collaboration between manufacturers, developers, and end-users can foster a secure IoT environment where devices can operate safely without jeopardizing network integrity.

4.3 Best Practices for Device Authentication

Implementing robust device authentication mechanisms is crucial in today's interconnected world where the volume of devices constantly increases, particularly with the rise of IoT. First and foremost, using unique device identifiers simplifies managing authentication, as every device receives a distinct ID. This identification can be combined with a secure credentialing system that requires proper encryption. Additionally, enforcing regular updates ensures that all devices use the latest security protocols and patches. It is also vital to configure devices to require authentication at multiple points: during setup, access attempts, and critical functions. Furthermore, establishing a device trust score can help prioritize security efforts, allowing organizations to monitor and validate connections continuously. This proactive approach helps in detecting unauthorized or suspicious devices before they can compromise the network.

Multi-factor authentication (MFA) plays a vital role in enhancing security beyond traditional username and password combinations. By requiring additional verification methods, such as a one-time code sent to a registered mobile device or the use of biometric identifiers, MFA significantly reduces the risk of unauthorized access. Cybersecurity professionals should consider integrating MFA into all layer levels, ensuring that any connection made by devices is authenticated thoroughly. Implementing adaptive MFA, which adjusts the authentication requirements based on contextual information, such as user behaviour and device risk factors, can further reinforce security without compromising user experience. In scenarios where critical data and systems are at stake, emphasizing the implementation of MFA not only provides an extra layer of security but also encourages a culture of security awareness within organizations.

The growth of IoT and cutting-edge devices prompts an evolving landscape of cyber threats. Consequently, it is essential for cybersecurity professionals to stay updated on the latest authentication technologies and techniques. Awareness of emerging standards and protocols, like OAuth 2.0 for authorization and FIDO2 for password less solutions, will drive better security practices forward. Cybersecurity teams should actively participate in information-sharing initiatives with vendors and peers across industries to improve collective security. Regular training sessions on the importance of device authentication for all employees can cultivate a culture of vigilance and accountability, which is often a line of defense against potential breaches. By embedding these practices into organizational policies, teams protect their infrastructure and enhance overall resilience against cyber threats.

5. Network Security for IoT

5.1 Secure Network Architecture for IoT

Designing a secure network architecture for Internet of Things (IoT) deployments requires a comprehensive understanding of various principles tailored to the unique challenges presented by connected devices. A fundamental tenet is the principle of least privilege, which emphasizes giving users and devices only the access necessary to perform their functions. This approach minimizes potential exposure and limits the impact of security breaches. Another important aspect is end-to-end encryption, which helps protect data as it travels across the network, ensuring that sensitive information is not easily intercepted or manipulated. Adoption of secure protocols such as TLS (Transport Layer Security) is also essential for safeguarding the communication between devices and the cloud or central management systems.

Furthermore, provisioning and authentication processes must be robust, incorporating techniques like multi-factor authentication and device identity management to ensure that only legitimate devices are allowed access to the network. Regular updates and patch management practices also play a critical role in maintaining security; keeping firmware and software up to date mitigates vulnerabilities that could be exploited by attackers. Effective logging and monitoring can provide insights into network activity, enabling the early detection of anomalies that could signify a security incident.

Segmentation and isolation are pivotal in reducing attack surfaces in an IoT environment. By segmenting the network, you can create distinct zones for different types of devices, which helps contain potential breaches. For example, devices used for critical functions, such as medical equipment or industrial controls, can be isolated from less secure devices, such as smart thermostats or consumer electronics. This limits the lateral movement of threats within the network. In practice, implementing firewalls and virtual LANs (VLANs) that separate traffic based on the sensitivity and role of the devices can substantially strengthen defenses. Additionally, applying micro-segmentation techniques ensures that even if one segment is compromised, it does not automatically grant access to the entire network infrastructure.

Ultimately, a well-thought-out secure network architecture for IoT not only incorporates these principles of design and segmentation but also fosters an environment of continuous security assessment. Regular risk assessments, vulnerability scanning, and penetration testing can help organizations better understand and mitigate their security posture, especially as new devices are integrated into their networks. Always remember to foster a culture of security awareness among all users, as human error can often be the weakest link in any security strategy.

5.2 Intrusion Detection Systems in IoT Networks

The effectiveness of intrusion detection systems (IDS) in identifying security threats within IoT networks cannot be overstated. As the number of connected devices grows exponentially, the unique challenges posed by these devices become increasingly apparent. Traditional security models often struggle to cope with the sheer volume and diversity of traffic generated by IoT devices. IDS plays a pivotal role in addressing these challenges by monitoring network traffic for unusual patterns or known malicious behaviour. Through the use of advanced techniques such as anomaly detection and signature-based detection, IDS can provide timely alerts and allow for quick responses to potential threats. These systems not only enhance security but also contribute valuable insights into the behaviour of devices, which is crucial for maintaining the integrity of IoT networks.

The integration of IDS with existing security frameworks further enhances visibility across the network landscape. By working in tandem with firewalls, security information and event management

(SIEM) solutions, and endpoint protection, IDS can create a comprehensive security posture. This integration allows for centralized monitoring, enabling security professionals to correlate events and better understand attack vectors. Additionally, leveraging machine learning algorithms within IDS systems can enhance response mechanisms by adapting to new threats in real-time, making it imperative for organizations to incorporate IDS into their broader security strategies. This holistic approach ensures that security teams are equipped with the tools needed to identify and mitigate emerging threats effectively.

To optimize the effectiveness of an IDS within an IoT network, it's crucial to ensure that the system is tailored to the specific environment. Settings and thresholds should reflect the unique behaviours of the devices in use, as well as the particular risks associated with those devices. Regular updates to the IDS signatures and anomaly models are essential to keep pace with evolving threats. Another practical approach is to foster continuous communication between different components of the security ecosystem, allowing for a more agile response capability. By maintaining a proactive stance and adapting to the dynamic nature of IoT deployments, organizations can significantly bolster their defences against potential intrusions.

5.3 Role of Firewalls in IoT Security

Firewalls serve as a critical line of defense in protecting IoT devices from unauthorized access. Because IoT devices are often less secure than traditional computing devices, they present unique vulnerabilities that can be targeted by cybercriminals. By deploying firewalls tailored to the specific needs of IoT environments, organizations can control traffic and establish a controlled access point for their connected devices. These firewalls can be implemented at both the network and device levels, allowing for the filtering of incoming and outgoing traffic based on predefined security rules. This preventive measure is essential in safeguarding sensitive data exchanged between IoT devices and external networks, effectively minimizing the attack surface available to malicious actors. The use of firewalls becomes even more imperative when considering that many IoT devices lack robust built-in security mechanisms.

Advanced firewall techniques are specifically designed to accommodate the diverse and often constrained nature of IoT environments. Traditional firewalls may not suffice due to the unique protocols and communication patterns associated with IoT devices. Stateful inspection, deep packet inspection, and application-level gateways become crucial. For example, stateful inspection allows firewalls to monitor the state of active connections and make decisions based on the context of traffic, rather than simply examining individual packets. Deep packet inspection goes further, analyzing the content of data packets to identify malicious patterns or unauthorized data exfiltration attempts. In addition, implementing behaviour-based firewalls can enhance security by continuously learning and adapting to network patterns, thus detecting deviations that may indicate security threats. These sophisticated techniques combine to form a multi-layered security strategy tailored to the nuances of IoT, ensuring that firewalls are not just barriers, but intelligent guardians of digital communication.

When configuring firewalls for IoT security, it's essential to adopt a risk-based approach that assesses the criticality of each device within the network. Not all IoT devices hold the same value or face the same threats, so prioritizing security measures based on this risk assessment can help allocate resources effectively. Additionally, regular updates and patch management should be part of the firewall strategy to address emerging threats and vulnerabilities. Cyber security professionals should also perform periodic audits and penetration testing to evaluate the effectiveness of the firewall deployment. Collaborating with IoT manufacturers and clearinghouses can provide insights into the best practices and emerging technologies relevant to securing IoT devices. By taking these proactive steps, organizations can create a dynamic defense mechanism that will evolve with the ever-changing landscape of IoT security.

6. Data Privacy and Protection in IoT

6.1 Challenges to Data Privacy in IoT

Pervasive data collection through the Internet of Things (IoT) presents critical challenges to data privacy. As devices increasingly become interconnected, vast amounts of personal and sensitive information are constantly being collected, analyzed, and transmitted. One significant challenge lies in the lack of transparency regarding what data is collected and how it is used. Users often remain uninformed about the extent of data gathering by their smart devices, leading to a breach of trust. Additionally, the sheer volume of data generated makes it difficult to apply strict data management and governance protocols, which is essential to ensuring privacy. With IoT devices often lacking robust security features, vulnerabilities become exposed, providing entry points for cybercriminals. Moreover, the diversity of IoT devices further complicates the standardization of privacy practices, as different manufacturers may implement varying levels of data protection. The inability to secure user data properly in an ecosystem filled with potentially untrustworthy devices represents a significant challenge. Furthermore, regulatory compliance issues arise, particularly when data is transferred across borders, which complicates efforts to ensure that data privacy standards are met consistently.

Insufficient privacy measures can lead to devastating data breaches, significantly compromising user trust in IoT ecosystems. Many IoT devices often have poor security configurations right out of the box. Weak default passwords, outdated firmware, and lack of user awareness about privacy settings contribute to vulnerabilities that can be exploited by attackers. When these devices are connected to wider networks, the potential consequences of a data breach increase exponentially. For example, unprotected cameras can allow unauthorized access to real-time video feeds, while health-related gadgets could expose sensitive medical information. Data breaches not only result in the loss of personal information but also carry financial repercussions for companies and individuals alike. Organizations may face hefty fines if found non-compliant with data protection regulations or suffer from reputational damage that can lead to a loss of customers. Due to the nature of IoT, where devices perpetually communicate with each other, a single breach can cascade into numerous systems being affected, further amplifying the risk and impact. This underscores the necessity of implementing strong, multi-layered security measures that encompass not just device-level protections but also network-level safeguards.

Amid these challenges, it is vital for cyber security professionals to prioritize comprehensive risk assessments tailored to IoT devices and their environments. By conducting regular audits and employing robust encryption methods, organizations can enhance data security while ensuring compliance with privacy regulations. Additionally, continuous education of users concerning the importance of strong passwords and active monitoring of their devices can alleviate some privacy concerns. This proactive approach helps build a security-conscious culture that helps mitigate risks associated with IoT proliferation.

6.2 Legal and Regulatory Considerations

The Internet of Things (IoT) poses unique challenges for data protection, largely due to the vast amounts of personal and sensitive information these devices collect. Various legal frameworks govern how organizations must handle this data to protect user privacy. The General Data Protection Regulation (GDPR) in Europe is one of the most stringent data protection laws. Under GDPR, organizations must ensure that personal data is processed lawfully, transparently, and for specific purposes. Individuals have the right to access their data, demand corrections, and even request deletion. This regulation places a distinct emphasis on data minimization and the protection of data subjects' rights, making it imperative for IoT deployments to incorporate mechanisms for compliance from the outset. Additionally, the California

Consumer Privacy Act (CCPA) sets important standards within the United States, providing California residents with rights regarding their personal information, including the right to know, the right to delete, and the right to opt-out of the sale of their data. These frameworks underline the necessity for organizations to adopt robust data protection measures that cater not only to compliance but also to the ethical handling of user information.

Compliance with regulations like GDPR and CCPA involves meeting a range of requirements that organizations must prioritize to ensure effective safeguarding of user data. Organizations are required to conduct data protection impact assessments (DPIAs) to identify and mitigate risks associated with their data processing activities. Moreover, transparency is crucial; organizations should maintain clear privacy notices that inform users about what data is being collected, how it will be used, and whom it may be shared with. Adopting a comprehensive data management strategy is not just about ticking boxes for compliance but involves implementing technical and organizational measures that encompass data security practices. This may include encryption, access controls, and regular audits of data processing activities, all of which establish a strong foundational posture against data breaches or misuse.

Considering the evolving nature of IoT technologies and their integration into various sectors, staying informed about legal and regulatory changes is vital. Cybersecurity professionals should leverage resources such as the European Data Protection Board's guidelines or the California Attorney General's suggestions for compliance under CCPA. These resources provide valuable insights into best practices and are crucial for developing an adaptable compliance framework. By systematically addressing these legal and regulatory considerations, organizations can not only protect user data effectively but also foster user trust in their IoT offerings, ensuring a secure, ethical digital environment.

6.3 Effective Data Protection Strategies

Implementing data protection measures within IoT systems is essential for safeguarding sensitive information. Security professionals need to understand the complexities of these systems, which often involve numerous interconnected devices. A comprehensive strategy should start with a thorough risk assessment, identifying potential vulnerabilities that could be exploited by malicious actors. Ensuring that devices have strong authentication protocols is vital. This includes using multifactor authentication and ensuring that default credentials are changed immediately upon deployment. Additionally, regular software updates and patch management must be prioritized to address known vulnerabilities. The architecture of the IoT system should also incorporate network segmentation, which limits the access and potential impact of a compromised device. Adopting a principle of least privilege is crucial; each device should only have the access necessary to perform its function. Regular audits and monitoring of network traffic can help detect anomalies that may indicate a data breach.

Data encryption and anonymization are two key practices that enhance data privacy across IoT systems. Encryption transforms data into a format that can only be read by individuals with the appropriate decryption keys. This ensures that even if data is intercepted, it remains unreadable to unauthorized users. Particularly in IoT environments, where data flows from devices to the cloud, strong encryption protocols, such as AES (Advanced Encryption Standard), should be employed for both data at rest and in transit. Anonymization, on the other hand, involves removing personally identifiable information from data sets, thus preserving privacy while still allowing for data analysis. Incorporating both practices can significantly mitigate the risks associated with data breaches and ensure compliance with regulations such as GDPR or HIPAA. Additionally, understanding and adopting relevant standards for encryption and anonymization will fortify an organization's data protection strategy effectively.

Another effective practice is to establish a robust incident response plan that prepares organizations for potential data breaches. This plan should include strategies for communication, containment, eradication, and recovery. Regularly conducting drills can ensure that all stakeholders are familiar with their responsibilities during a security incident. It's also beneficial to foster a culture of security awareness across the organization. Training employees about the potential risks associated with IoT devices and data handling can significantly reduce human error, which is often a contributing factor to security breaches. Organizations should also collaborate with industry peers to share knowledge and insights about emerging threats related to IoT devices. Staying informed about the latest security technologies, such as blockchain for secure data transactions, contributes to a more resilient data protection framework.

7. Incident Response and Management in IoT

7.1 Developing an Incident Response Plan for IoT

Creating an incident response plan for IoT environments involves understanding the unique challenges posed by a multitude of interconnected devices. Essential components of this plan must include identification of critical assets, assessment of vulnerabilities, and the establishment of a clear communication strategy. Begin by cataloging all IoT devices in your network, noting their applications, potential weaknesses, and data they collect. This asset inventory allows for prioritization based on risk assessment. Integrate virtualization and segmentation strategies to limit the impact of incidents. Your incident response team should have defined roles, with a robust chain of command that addresses both technical and operational concerns. Additionally, workflows for incident detection, investigation, containment, eradication, and recovery should be clearly laid out. Establishing procedures for logging and documenting incidents enhances accountability and supports post-incident analysis, which is crucial for improving future responses.

Regular testing and updating of the incident response plan is vital to ensure its effectiveness. Real-world scenarios change quickly, especially in the realm of IoT, where new vulnerabilities can emerge as technologies evolve. Conducting frequent drills simulating incidents will help to validate the plan's effectiveness and assess team readiness. During these exercises, evaluate the response times and effectiveness of the communication protocols established in the plan. Consistently review and revise the incident response plan in light of new insights gained from these drills, as well as from lessons learned during actual incidents. Keeping the plan up-to-date is not just about adapting to technological changes; it includes being responsive to changes in regulatory requirements and threat landscapes that impact your organization.

A practical tip for maintaining an effective incident response plan is to create a dedicated communication channel that is secure and accessible to team members during an incident. This channel should allow for real-time information sharing and decision-making. By ensuring that every team member can access critical information quickly, you enhance your organization's ability to respond to incidents effectively, regardless of the type or severity. Bear in mind that preparedness is an ongoing process, and continual refinement of both technology and human involvement in these plans is key to addressing the ever-evolving nature of IoT security.

7.2 Forensics in IoT Security Breaches

Conducting digital forensics on IoT devices in the event of security breaches involves a nuanced and methodical approach. One of the first steps is to secure the device to prevent any further data alteration. This may involve physically isolating the affected device from the network and powering it down if necessary. Forensic investigators must utilize specialized tools to capture a bit-by-bit image of the device's storage, ensuring that the original data remains intact for further analysis. Analyzing the captured data can include checking log files for unauthorized access, identifying malware or suspicious applications, and recovering deleted files that may contain critical evidence. Furthermore, understanding the proprietary nature of many IoT devices complicates this process, as different manufacturers may have unique operating systems and firmware, which can obscure crucial forensic indicators. Nonetheless, industry-standard tools such as Autopsy, FTK Imager, and EnCase can aid in the examination of IoT devices, enabling investigators to navigate these complexities.

The legal and ethical considerations involved in IoT forensics are fundamental for cybersecurity professionals. Adhering to legal protocols is critical; unauthorized access or mishandling of data can lead to significant legal implications, including potential charges of tampering with evidence. It is essential to establish a clear chain of custody for all collected data, documenting every step taken during the forensic process. Additionally, ethical considerations come into play, particularly regarding user privacy. Many IoT devices collect sensitive personal information, and it is vital to approach investigations with respect for individual rights. Data protection regulations, such as the General Data Protection Regulation (GDPR) in Europe, impose strict guidelines on how personal data should be handled, making compliance non-negotiable during forensic analysis. Failure to observe these legal and ethical standards can not only compromise the integrity of the investigation but can also result in erosion of public trust in cybersecurity practices.

To enhance the effectiveness of IoT forensics, it's advisable for professionals to stay updated on technological advancements and evolving legal frameworks. Continuous education and training on new forensic tools designed for IoT devices, along with an understanding of legal updates, can significantly improve response times and outcomes in security breach situations. Building strong partnerships with legal counsel familiar with cyber law can also provide guidance through complex scenarios. Staying informed about emerging threats and vulnerabilities within the IoT landscape will empower cybersecurity professionals to develop proactive measures, ensuring that forensic methodologies remain robust and effective. Keeping abreast of industry standards and best practices is essential for maintaining a security posture capable of addressing the unique challenges posed by IoT environments.

7.3 Learning from IoT Security Incidents

Conducting post-incident analysis is an essential practice for any organization dealing with IoT technology. The rapid proliferation of connected devices has led to increasingly sophisticated cyber threats, making it crucial to evaluate security incidents thoroughly. This analysis helps identify vulnerabilities and weaknesses in existing security measures, enabling organizations to bolster their defences against future attacks. By dissecting each incident, organizations can uncover not only the technical failings that allowed the breach to occur but also the human factors at play, such as insufficient training or flawed protocols. This understanding fosters a culture of continuous improvement within teams, as lessons learned from these experiences can shape future security policies, upgrade protocols, and enhance risk assessment processes. A robust post-incident review process not only strengthens the organization's cybersecurity posture but also builds resilience and trust with users and stakeholders.

Case studies of notable IoT security incidents reveal valuable insights that extend beyond technical specifications. For instance, examining high-profile breaches sheds light on common attack vectors and the tactics employed by malicious actors. In one such incident, a smart thermostat was compromised due to a weak default password, highlighting the critical need for manufacturers to enforce stricter password policies and configure devices for better security out of the box. Another example involves a connected home security system that was undermined by lacklustre encryption practices, allowing attackers to intercept communication between devices. This emphasizes the importance of implementing robust encryption standards to safeguard data integrity. Each case study provides an opportunity to analyze response efforts, recovery strategies, and communication with affected users, which can ultimately guide organizations in developing proactive measures and refining incident response plans. Learning from these incidents promotes a deeper understanding of IoT security, encouraging the adoption of comprehensive, layered defences.

As the landscape of connected devices continues to evolve, it is imperative for cybersecurity professionals to actively engage in assessing and applying lessons learned from past incidents. Regularly conducting tabletop exercises simulating different attack scenarios can prepare teams for the dynamic nature of IoT threats. Additionally, collaboration with industry peers on shared experiences fosters knowledge exchange that can lead to innovative security solutions and quicker recovery times. Emphasizing the importance of user education and awareness is also paramount; organizations should prioritize initiatives that inform customers about securing their own devices and networks. By taking these actionable steps, cybersecurity professionals can not only enhance their organizational security posture but also contribute to a more secure and resilient IoT ecosystem overall.

8. The Role of AI and Machine Learning in IoT Security

8.1 Leveraging AI for Threat Detection

Artificial intelligence is becoming a critical tool for enhancing the detection of threats within Internet of Things (IoT) systems. As the number of connected devices increases, so does the potential attack surface, making traditional security measures insufficient. AI can assist in real-time monitoring of these devices, automatically analyzing vast amounts of data generated by IoT networks. Machine learning algorithms can be trained to recognize normal behaviour patterns for devices and trigger alerts when deviations occur. These intelligent systems can continuously learn from new data, improving accuracy over time and adapting to evolving threats. By leveraging AI, cybersecurity professionals can gain a more comprehensive view of the threat landscape, allowing for proactive security measures rather than reactive responses.

The algorithms utilized in AI for threat detection focus on identifying anomalies and potential security breaches within IoT ecosystems. Common techniques employed include supervised and unsupervised learning models. Supervised learning involves training algorithms on datasets labeled with known threats, enabling them to predict potential future breaches. Conversely, unsupervised learning allows algorithms to analyze data without prior labels, identifying irregular patterns that could indicate malicious activity. Techniques such as clustering, which groups similar data points, can highlight unusual device behaviour, while decision trees and neural networks refine responses based on historical data. Furthermore, deep learning methods, which mimic human brain functions, are particularly effective in processing complex datasets typical of IoT environments, providing enhanced detection capabilities.

Implementing AI effectively requires an understanding of the unique challenges presented by IoT systems. Keeping up with the rapid pace of technological advancement is crucial for security professionals. Ensuring that AI models are regularly updated with current data is vital for maintaining their effectiveness. In addition to adaptive learning, integrating threat intelligence feeds can provide essential context for identifying unusual patterns. As the future unfolds, the collaboration between AI technologies and cybersecurity practices will be the cornerstone of developing robust defense mechanisms against increasingly sophisticated attacks. Continually refining these systems while investing in staff training on AI capabilities will ensure organizations remain ahead of emerging threats.

8.2 Machine Learning Techniques for IoT Security

Machine learning methods are becoming increasingly vital in the field of Internet of Things (IoT) security, as they provide advanced capabilities to detect and respond to potential threats. Various algorithms, such as decision trees, neural networks, and clustering techniques, are utilized in identifying patterns and anomalies in data generated by IoT devices. These methods facilitate real-time analysis of network traffic and user behaviour's across connected devices. For instance, supervised learning models can be trained using historical data to recognize normal operational patterns, allowing for the timely identification of deviations that may indicate a security breach. Furthermore, unsupervised learning techniques can discover new threats by identifying unusual behaviour's without requiring pre-defined labels, thus adapting to previously unseen risks.

The effectiveness of these machine learning techniques in adapting to evolving security threats lies in their ability to learn from new data continuously. As malware and attack methodologies grow increasingly sophisticated, static security measures often fall short. In contrast, adaptive machine learning systems can refine their algorithms based on new input, enabling them to evolve alongside emerging threats. For example, ensemble learning techniques combine multiple models to enhance detection accuracy by amalgamating diverse perspectives of data. Moreover, reinforcement learning is particularly promising, as it allows systems to make decisions based on rewards, continuously improving their responses to security incidents over time. This ability to self-adjust and enhance situational awareness is crucial for maintaining the integrity of IoT networks against dynamic and diverse threats.

Cyber security professionals must consider the integration of machine learning techniques into their IoT security frameworks thoughtfully. Implementing a comprehensive approach requires not only advanced algorithms but also an understanding of the specific environment and devices in use. Regularly updating training data and continuously monitoring system performance are key strategies. Establishing clear communication channels among devices and incorporating feedback mechanisms can optimize detection processes. As threats continue to evolve, leveraging machine learning's adaptive capabilities will remain essential in fortifying IoT infrastructure against cyber risks.

8.3 Ethical Considerations in AI-Driven Security

The integration of artificial intelligence in IoT security and data handling brings forth significant ethical implications that demand careful consideration. As AI continues to evolve and become more prevalent in managing security protocols, the potential for bias in algorithms poses a serious concern. AI systems can inadvertently learn from flawed data sets, leading to skewed decision-making that may compromise the integrity of security processes. In scenarios where AI determines access to sensitive information or the response to a detected threat, the consequences of these biases can be critical. Additionally, the automation of surveillance through AI raises questions about privacy and consent. Users may be monitored without their awareness, blurring the line between security and infringement on personal freedoms. Thus, it is essential for cybersecurity professionals to scrutinize the underlying frameworks of AI systems to ensure that ethical standards are met while aligning with legal requirements.

Establishing guidelines for the responsible use of AI in security is crucial to mitigate these ethical concerns. These guidelines should encompass transparency, accountability, and fairness to ensure that AI-driven security solutions do not exacerbate existing inequalities or create new vulnerabilities. By promoting transparency, organizations can enhance trust among users who rely on these technologies for their security. This can be achieved by making the workings of AI systems understandable and accessible. Accountability is equally important; organizations must have clear policies regarding who is responsible for the decisions made by AI. This includes ensuring that there is a human oversight aspect so that AI does not operate in a vacuum where errors can go unaddressed. Finally, fairness must be core to AI deployment, which means ongoing evaluations must be conducted to assess the performance of AI systems to avoid discrimination. Creating a robust framework that incorporates these elements will not only bolster ethical practices in AI utilization but also foster a safer environment for users and organizations alike.

As the landscape of AI and IoT technology continues to evolve, it is vital for cybersecurity professionals to stay informed about emerging ethical considerations. Engaging in continuous education and dialogue about the implications of AI can enhance decision-making and lead to better security outcomes. Consider benchmarking against established ethical standards and actively participating in forums where these critical issues are discussed, as collaboration can lead to innovative solutions that benefit the industry as a whole. Thoughtful approaches to ethical AI deployment will shape the future of security in a way that not only protects assets but also upholds the rights of individuals.

9. Future Trends in IoT and Cyber Security

9.1 Evolution of IoT Architecture

The evolution of Internet of Things (IoT) architectures is primarily driven by the relentless pace of technological advancement and the burgeoning requirements of interconnected devices. As these devices become smarter and more capable, IoT architectures must adapt to accommodate greater data generation and processing needs while being responsive to emerging challenges. Traditional centralized systems are gradually giving way to more decentralized approaches, where data processing is done closer to the source. This shift is crucial not only for enhancing responsiveness and reducing latency but also for addressing privacy and security concerns that typically arise with the massive data collected by IoT devices. As various industry sectors adopt IoT solutions, they face unique demands, prompting developers to innovate specific architectural frameworks tailored to those needs. More scalable, flexible, and hierarchical architectures are emerging, paving the way for future-proof IoT systems that can efficiently manage diverse applications across different environments.

The roles of cloud, edge, and fog computing in future IoT ecosystems are pivotal. Cloud computing serves as a backbone for data storage and heavy computational tasks, allowing for virtually limitless scalability. However, as more devices connect and generate a continuous stream of data, the limitations of relying solely on the cloud become evident, particularly concerning latency and bandwidth. Edge computing addresses these challenges by processing data closer to where it is generated, which significantly reduces latency and conserves bandwidth by filtering and aggregating data before it transits to the cloud. This local processing minimizes the amount of data transmitted and enables real-time responses, critical for tasks that demand immediate action. Fog computing extends the concept of edge computing by adding an additional layer, distributing resources, services, and applications across a network that stretches from the edge to the cloud. This multi-tiered approach can provide better resource management, optimize service delivery, and enhance security, ensuring a more resilient IoT architecture that is well-suited for the complexities of future technological demands.

As you navigate the evolving landscape of IoT architectures, staying informed about advancements in cloud, edge, and fog computing will be essential in effectively addressing the unique security challenges they present. Keeping an eye on developments in these domains will empower cyber security professionals to guide their organizations in implementing robust security measures tailored to the specific needs of both centralized and distributed IoT systems.

9.2 Predicting Future Security Challenges

The Internet of Things (IoT) is rapidly expanding, bringing new devices, applications, and services into our daily lives. This growth introduces a range of emerging security challenges that cybersecurity professionals must identify and address. As more devices become interconnected, the attack surface for potential breaches increases significantly. Vulnerabilities in one device can create a cascading effect that compromises entire networks. IoT devices often have limited processing power and memory, making them inherently less secure. Additionally, many of these devices are deployed in environments where they might not receive regular updates or security patches, leading to outdated software and increased risk. Phishing attacks targeting smart home devices, unauthorized access to IoT ecosystems, and the potential for large-scale distributed denial of service (DDoS) attacks utilizing compromised devices are just a few examples of the emerging threats that organizations must be prepared to face.

To mitigate these future threats, organizations need to adopt proactive measures that strengthen their security posture. Firstly, implementing a robust security framework that encompasses the entire lifecycle of IoT devices—from design and deployment to maintenance and retirement—is essential. This includes adopting secure coding practices, conducting thorough security assessments before deployment, and ensuring that all devices are capable of receiving updates throughout their operational lifespan. Furthermore, organizations should prioritize network segmentation to isolate IoT devices from critical systems, thereby minimizing the impact of a potential breach. Continuous monitoring of network traffic can also help detect anomalies that may indicate a security incident in real time. Finally, fostering a culture of security awareness among employees and stakeholders is crucial. Regular training sessions that emphasize the importance of security best practices can reinforce the need for vigilance and proactive behaviour against potential threats.

Monitoring and assessing the cybersecurity landscape as IoT technology evolves will be key to staying ahead of emerging challenges. Organizations should invest in threat intelligence tools that provide insights into the latest vulnerabilities and attack trends specific to IoT devices. Furthermore, collaborating with industry peers and participating in information-sharing initiatives can enhance collective knowledge and defences against evolving threats. Leverage advanced analytics and machine learning to improve anomaly detection capabilities, as these technologies can identify patterns that human analysts might miss. By taking these steps, organizations can not only protect their own systems but also contribute to a more secure IoT ecosystem overall. Regularly revisiting security strategies and adapting to changes in technology will ensure resilience against future cyber threats.

9.3 Emerging Technologies Impacting IoT Security

Emerging technologies are significantly reshaping the landscape of IoT security, with blockchain at the forefront of these innovations. Blockchain provides a decentralized framework that allows IoT devices to communicate and transact without relying on a central authority. This decentralization is crucial for mitigating single points of failure, which are susceptible to attacks that could compromise or disrupt entire networks. By utilizing smart contracts, IoT devices can execute automated and secure transactions, ensuring that data integrity and authenticity are preserved without requiring extensive manual intervention. Additionally, the immutability of blockchain records ensures that any unauthorized changes to data can be easily identified, providing a solid layer of security for sensitive information transmitted through IoT applications. The integration of machine learning and artificial intelligence also plays a crucial role. These technologies enable advanced data analytics that can predict and identify unusual patterns of behaviour, signalling potential security breaches before they escalate into serious threats. Together, these cutting-edge technologies offer a transformative approach that enhances both the resilience and security of IoT systems.

The implementation of these technologies can greatly enhance the trust and security levels in IoT applications. By establishing a foundation of transparency and accountability through blockchain, stakeholders can engage with IoT devices knowing that their data is secure. Each device on the network can be monitored for compliance, ensuring that they do not harbour vulnerabilities that could be exploited. By employing machine learning algorithms to assess the health of the devices, organizations can achieve proactive identification of threats, allowing for real-time responses to suspicious activities. This predictive capability reduces reliance on reactive measures, transforming the approach to security from a response-based model to a prevention-focused paradigm. Furthermore, the interoperability offered by blockchain can facilitate global collaboration among entities that utilize IoT in various sectors, promoting a broader effort to ensure security standards are met across different industries. As cyber threats continually evolve, staying ahead of potential vulnerabilities becomes imperative. Implementing these emerging technologies will not only bolster the security of individual IoT ecosystems but also contribute to creating a more secure digital infrastructure as a whole.

Leveraging these technologies requires a thorough understanding of both the technical capabilities and the contextual implications of IoT networks. Cyber security professionals should actively pursue knowledge about advancements in blockchain, machine learning, and their integration into IoT devices.

Keeping abreast of industry trends and collaborating with peers will facilitate a more robust security posture. Furthermore, investing in continuous education and training for personnel involved in IoT development and security will ensure that an organization is well-prepared to tackle the complexities that arise in this rapidly changing field. By fostering this environment of learning and adaptation, organizations can effectively mitigate risks and enhance the security and trustworthiness of their IoT implementations.

10. Best Practices for IoT Security

10.1 Security by Design Principles

Integrating security into the design phase of IoT devices is critical for protecting sensitive information and maintaining user trust. As IoT devices become pervasive, they are increasingly targeted by malicious actors. A device that is not designed with security in mind can provide an entry point into larger networks, leading to data breaches and operational disruption. It is essential to understand that security is not just an afterthought or a patch to be added later; it must be an integral part of the device from its inception. Developers should prioritize the identification of potential vulnerabilities and ensure that robust security measures are embedded within the device's architecture. This proactive approach mitigates risks and minimizes the impact of any security breaches that may occur.

Key principles of security by design include adopting a "least privilege" approach where devices have only the permissions absolutely necessary for their functions. This limits the potential damage that can occur if a device is compromised. Incorporating encryption throughout the data transmission process is essential to safeguard data integrity and confidentiality. Regular software updates and patches must be planned to quickly address newly discovered vulnerabilities, thus ensuring ongoing protection against evolving threats. Additionally, implementing user authentication mechanisms fortifies access control, ensuring that only authorized entities interact with the device. Another vital principle is to maintain transparency, allowing users to understand how their data is handled and stored. When these security principles are adhered to during the design phase, they significantly enhance the resilience of IoT devices against cyber-attacks.

One practical tip for enhancing security by design involves conducting threat modeling during the initial stages of development. By identifying potential threats and vulnerabilities early, teams can design countermeasures that are built into the architecture rather than added on later. This holistic approach not only enhances security but also streamlines compliance with various industry regulations that govern data protection. Integrating feedback from security experts can further strengthen the design, creating more reliable and secure IoT devices that withstand the test of time.

10.2 Developing Secure Applications for IoT

Developing secure applications for the Internet of Things (IoT) requires a strategic approach tailored to the unique challenges posed by interconnected devices. To start, it is essential to prioritize security at every stage of the development lifecycle. This means including security assessments in the design phase, implementing robust authentication and authorization methods, and ensuring that data encryption is standard practice. Applications should minimize data exposure by collecting only necessary information and using secure protocols for data transmission. Continuously monitoring the security posture of IoT devices can further enhance the development of secure applications, which should include regular updates and patches. Utilizing frameworks that focus on security can help establish a strong foundation, enabling developers to proactively address vulnerabilities before they can be exploited.

The necessity of regular security assessments and updates cannot be overstated in the context of IoT. Given the rapid evolution of technology and the constant emergence of new threats, systems must be designed to adapt. Regular security assessments should encompass not only the applications but also the devices and networks they interact with. Implementing automated tools for vulnerability scanning can provide ongoing insights into potential weaknesses. Moreover, maintaining a routine schedule for software updates and patches is crucial. Timely updates can significantly reduce the risk of exploitation from known vulnerabilities, and incorporating a robust incident response mechanism will allow for quick action if a breach occurs. This proactive approach ensures that security is not just a one-time setup but a continuously evolving process.

Keeping in mind these guidelines, developers must focus not only on the creation of secure applications but also on fostering a culture of security within their teams. Educating developers about potential threats and secure coding practices will build a more resilient application ecosystem. They should remain vigilant against evolving attack vectors, and adopt a mindset that considers security as a fundamental aspect of application development, rather than an afterthought. Incorporating these best practices not only fortifies individual applications but also contributes to the overall security landscape of IoT, protecting users and their sensitive data. One practical tip is to integrate security tools early in the application development process; doing so can save considerable time and resources later, resulting in a more robust and secure end product.

10.3 Continuous Monitoring and Improvement

Continuous monitoring is a cornerstone of maintaining IoT security. The landscape of connected devices is evolving rapidly, presenting new vulnerabilities that can be exploited if left unchecked. As cyber threats become increasingly sophisticated, organizations must not only implement security measures but also monitor their effectiveness on an ongoing basis. Failing to do so can lead to gaps that attackers can use to breach systems. Continuous monitoring enables security professionals to detect anomalies in real time, maintain the integrity of their networks, and respond swiftly to potential threats. Establishing a feedback loop that constantly assesses the security posture of IoT devices helps ensure that organizations stay ahead of the curve, fortifying their defences as new challenges arise.

To effectively monitor and refine security protocols over time, organizations should adopt a comprehensive approach that includes various methodologies. One effective strategy is the integration of automated tools that utilize machine learning and artificial intelligence. These tools can analyze vast amounts of data from connected devices, identifying patterns and flagging unusual behaviour's that may indicate a security breach. Furthermore, regular penetration testing and vulnerability assessments should be conducted to evaluate the robustness of security protocols. Engaging in continuous training for personnel involved in security measures is equally important, ensuring that they remain informed about the evolving threat landscape and best practices in IoT security. By fostering a culture of ongoing improvement, organizations can adapt their security strategies to counteract emerging threats effectively.

Staying proactive in the realm of IoT security requires a commitment to continuous learning and adaptation. It is critical for cybersecurity professionals to engage in regular assessments of their security strategies, including reviewing current protocols against industry standards and updating them as necessary. This approach not only reduces the risk of breaches but also instils confidence in stakeholders regarding the organization's commitment to securing sensitive information. As IoT technology continues to expand, developing a structured framework for continuous monitoring and improvement will be essential in maintaining security resilience and fostering trust in connected ecosystems.

11. Regulatory Compliance and Standards for IoT Security

11.1 Overview of IoT Security Standards

The landscape of Internet of Things (IoT) security is governed by a range of standards that aim to establish best practices for securing devices and their communications. Notable among these are the ISO/IEC 27001, which provides a framework for information security management systems; the NIST Cybersecurity Framework, designed to guide organizations in managing cybersecurity risk; and the OWASP IoT Top Ten, which highlights the most critical security vulnerabilities in IoT devices. Each of these standards helps organizations understand the necessary protocols, technical measures, and risk management processes required to secure their connected devices, ensuring that they can withstand potential breaches and attacks. Moreover, these standards evolve continuously, adapting to emerging threats and technologies in the IoT domain.

The implications of these standards extend beyond mere compliance; they fundamentally influence how manufacturers and developers approach IoT device security. For manufacturers, adherence to these standards can enhance product reputation and customer trust, including considerations for secure design, testing, and ongoing updates. It can also streamline the development process by providing clear guidelines for security measures, ultimately reducing vulnerabilities at the outset. For developers, these standards inform the coding practices and infrastructure designs necessary to create resilient applications. The adoption of such standards often results in a competitive advantage in the marketplace, as consumers increasingly demand trustworthy and safe connected devices.

Cybersecurity professionals working with IoT should remain vigilant about the latest standards and frameworks, as these will inform not only the security posture of current implementations but also shape the trajectory of future innovations. Understanding these standards allows for proactive measures in risk assessment and mitigation, ensuring robust devices that can effectively communicate and operate within the network without introducing significant vulnerabilities. Investing time in mastering these standards can lead to more secure and resilient IoT ecosystems.

11.2 Compliance Challenges and Solutions

Organizations increasingly face a multitude of challenges in achieving compliance with the evolving Internet of Things (IoT) standards. One of the primary hurdles is the sheer diversity of devices and platforms that businesses need to integrate. IoT encompasses a wide range of devices, from smart sensors in manufacturing to connected medical devices in healthcare. Each of these devices often adheres to different compliance requirements, making it difficult for organizations to establish a unified compliance strategy. Additionally, the rapid pace of technological advancement means standards can change frequently, leaving organizations scrambling to adjust their compliance frameworks. Data management also presents significant challenges. IoT devices typically generate vast amounts of data, and ensuring that this data is collected, stored, and processed in compliance with regulations such as GDPR or HIPAA can overwhelm existing compliance processes. Organizations often struggle to maintain visibility over this data, complicating audits and compliance checks.

To navigate these challenges, organizations can implement several solutions and tools designed to facilitate compliance efforts. Establishing a centralized compliance management system can streamline the monitoring of various regulations and IoT standards. This system should incorporate automated compliance checks that continuously assess device activity and data usage against predefined standards. Leveraging advanced analytics and machine learning can also help organizations identify compliance gaps and predict potential future risks. Investing in training for staff about IoT-specific compliance measures is crucial. This not only equips teams with the necessary knowledge to manage compliance but also fosters a culture of compliance throughout the organization. Additionally, collaborating with third-party vendors that specialize in IoT compliance can provide organizations with the expertise needed to navigate the complex landscape of standards and regulations effectively. Utilizing frameworks such as the NIST Cybersecurity Framework can guide organizations through the integration of security and compliance measures specific to IoT environments.

Staying up to date with the latest IoT standards and regulations is imperative. Regularly reviewing and recalibrating compliance strategies can help organizations remain resilient in an ever-changing environment. It is essential to build flexibility into compliance frameworks, as this allows for swift adaptations when regulations are updated or new devices are incorporated into the network. Establishing an ongoing feedback loop from both compliance monitoring and staff training can further enhance compliance efforts, ensuring that the organization is always aligned with the best practices in IoT compliance.

11.3 Best Practices for Achieving Compliance

Organizations must implement effective practices to ensure compliance with security standards, especially in the context of rapidly evolving technologies such as the Internet of Things (IoT). A fundamental practice involves establishing a robust governance framework that clearly delineates roles and responsibilities within the organization. This framework should be supported by policies and procedures that reflect both internal objectives and external regulations. Engaging all stakeholders, from executive management to operational teams, ensures that compliance becomes a shared responsibility. Furthermore, continuous training and awareness programs help employees understand the significance of compliance and recognize their part in maintaining security standards. Regularly revisiting and updating these policies is also essential as technologies and threats evolve.

Regular audits and assessments play a critical role in maintaining compliance by providing insights into the current security posture and identifying areas for improvement. Conducting these assessments on a scheduled basis allows organizations to not only comply with regulatory demands but also to ensure that they remain resilient against potential threats. External audits by third-party vendors can offer an objective view, highlighting gaps that internal teams may overlook. By leveraging automated tools, organizations can streamline the audit process and gain real-time visibility into compliance metrics. Post-assessment, it's crucial to develop action plans that address identified issues promptly, fostering a culture of accountability and proactive risk management.

In an era where connectivity is fundamental, ensuring compliance should be regarded as an ongoing process rather than a one-time achievement. A practical tip for organizations is to integrate compliance considerations into their technology development lifecycle. This means that from the inception of a new device or technology, considerations for security standards and regulatory compliance should be part of the design and implementation phases. By doing so, organizations not only streamline their processes but also help mitigate risks before products even reach the market.

12. Building a Cyber Security Culture for IoT

12.1 Employee Training and Awareness

Training employees to recognize and respond to IoT security threats is crucial in today's interconnected landscape. With the rising adoption of IoT devices, vulnerabilities increase, and employees become the first line of defense against potential breaches. It is essential for staff members to understand the nature of these threats, from data interception to unauthorized device access. Regular workshops and training sessions can empower employees to identify suspicious activities, such as unusual network connections or unrecognized devices, thereby mitigating risks before they escalate. Hands-on training that includes simulations of IoT-related incidents can also prepare employees to respond swiftly and effectively, ensuring that they are not only aware but also equipped to handle real-life scenarios. By fostering a proactive mindset towards security, organizations can dramatically strengthen their overall defense mechanisms against IoT vulnerabilities.

Fostering a culture of security awareness within the organization is equally important for long-term sustainability in cybersecurity efforts. To create this culture, leadership must engage every level of the organization, from top executives to frontline employees. Establishing clear communication channels regarding security policies and best practices can encourage an environment where questions and concerns are welcomed. Regular updates on evolving threats, tailored to the varying levels of technical insight across different teams, ensure that everyone remains informed. Additionally, recognizing and rewarding employees who demonstrate strong security practices can reinforce desired behaviors and encourage ongoing vigilance. Integrating security awareness into the onboarding process for new employees and conducting periodic refreshers for existing staff can make security an ingrained part of the organizational culture. This, in turn, creates an engaged workforce that views cybersecurity as a shared responsibility and not solely the burden of the IT department.

A practical tip for enhancing security awareness is to implement a behavioural assessment tool that tracks employee interactions with IoT devices and networks. By analyzing how employees engage with these elements, organizations can identify common pitfalls and areas requiring additional training. Tailoring training programs based on these insights can lead to more effective education and a strengthened security posture across the organization.

12.2 Creating Policies for IoT Security

Organizations face significant challenges in ensuring the security of IoT devices due to the sheer number and variety of these devices connected to networks. Clear and enforceable policies are vital to mitigating risks associated with IoT environments. These policies should outline best practices for the secure deployment and management of devices, ensuring that all stakeholders understand their responsibilities. This is essential not only for compliance but also to establish a culture of security that permeates the organization. By defining standards for device authentication, data protection, network segmentation, and incident response, organizations can create a robust framework to safeguard their IoT infrastructure against evolving threats.

Drafting effective IoT security policies requires a thorough understanding of an organization's specific needs and existing cybersecurity framework. Begin by identifying the potential risks and vulnerabilities associated with IoT devices in your network. Engage with relevant stakeholders, including IT, security, and business units, to ensure the policies are comprehensive and practical. Describe clear procedures for device onboarding, regular updates, and user training to ensure everyone is clear on operations. Implementing these policies involves not just documentation, but also consistent enforcement and monitoring. Regularly review and update your policies to adapt to the ever-changing technological landscape and emerging threats. A proactive approach to policy implementation will help create a resilient environment for IoT devices while maintaining operational efficiency.

It's essential to provide ongoing training and resources to employees, ensuring they understand the policies and their role in maintaining IoT security. Establish metrics to evaluate the effectiveness of these policies, enabling continuous improvement. Document incidents and responses to refine the policies over time. Consider establishing a feedback loop involving users and security personnel to identify areas for improvement or adaptation. Implementing strong IoT security policies does not only protect your network but also enhances the overall security posture of your organization.

12.3 Fostering a Security Mindset in Organizations

Instilling a proactive security mindset across all organizational levels is crucial, especially as IoT devices become more integrated into our networks. To achieve this, organizations must weave security into the fabric of their everyday operations. This starts with education and awareness. Training programs tailored to different roles within the organization can significantly enhance understanding of security risks and the responsibilities each individual has in mitigating them. Regular workshops and simulations that illustrate real-world cyber threats can engage employees at all levels, prompting them to think critically about security in their daily activities.

Leadership plays a pivotal role in promoting security best practices. Leaders must model the behaviour's they wish to see by prioritizing security in their decision-making processes and resource allocation. This involves establishing clear security policies and demonstrating a commitment to compliance. Visibility is key; when leadership openly discusses security topics, it emphasizes their importance and encourages a culture where security is everyone's responsibility. By embracing open communication about security challenges and successes, leaders can foster an environment where employees feel empowered to report issues and share ideas, thereby enhancing the overall security posture of the organization.

To maintain momentum in fostering a security mindset, organizations can implement continuous improvement strategies. Regular assessments and feedback loops help ensure that security practices remain relevant as technology evolves. Incorporating security metrics into performance evaluations can reinforce the importance of these practices and keep them front-of-mind. Ultimately, creating an environment where security is seen as a collective responsibility rather than a checkbox can significantly strengthen the organization's defense against evolving cyber threats.

13. Collaboration and Information Sharing in IoT Security

13.1 Importance of Collaboration Among Stakeholders

Collaboration between manufacturers, users, and regulatory bodies is critical for ensuring the security and effectiveness of Internet of Things (IoT) devices. Manufacturers alone cannot secure their products in isolation; the nuanced environments where these devices operate require input from a variety of stakeholders. Users must actively communicate their experiences, pain points, and security concerns, while regulatory bodies need to establish guidelines that reflect the evolving landscape of technology. These dialogues foster an ecosystem where industry standards can be developed, ensuring that security is built in from the ground up rather than being an afterthought. When manufacturers, users, and regulators work together, the likelihood of developing robust solutions that address potential vulnerabilities increases significantly, ultimately enhancing overall trust in IoT technologies.

Shared information among these stakeholders plays a vital role in improving the overall IoT security posture. By exchanging data regarding vulnerabilities, incident reports, and best practices, all parties can be better informed, allowing for more rapid innovation and adaptation to emerging threats. For instance, when manufacturers gain insights into specific threats faced by users through real-world experiences, they can prioritize necessary updates and patches. Users, on their part, should actively report incidents and cooperate with manufacturers to help refine security measures. Regulatory bodies can assist by creating frameworks for sharing information safely, ensuring that sensitive data is protected while still enabling comprehensive threat assessments. Such openness not only promotes a culture of collaboration but also leads to a more resilient IoT ecosystem capable of withstanding and adapting to the challenges of modern cyber threats.

To strengthen this collaborative environment, stakeholders should engage in regular forums or workshops aimed at discussing best practices and lessons learned in IoT security. Companies could benefit from participating in shared research initiatives that assess common vulnerabilities across devices and applications. These endeavours may help to identify gaps in security solutions, driving innovation and enhancing overall device integrity. The proactive exchange of knowledge and ideas not only nurtures relationships among stakeholders but also creates a unified front against potential threats to the future of IoT connectivity.

13.2 Platforms for Information Sharing

Numerous platforms and frameworks have emerged to facilitate information sharing specifically focused on IoT security. These platforms vary in scope and capability, each designed to address the unique challenges posed by the integration of IoT devices within existing networks. Well-known frameworks such as the IoT Security Foundation and the Industrial Internet Consortium provide structured approaches to security best practices, guidelines, and frameworks tailored to enhance information sharing across organizations. Additionally, collaborative platforms like the Open Web Application Security Project (OWASP) have created dedicated resources and tools aimed at improving the security of IoT devices by sharing vulnerability information and mitigation strategies. This collaborative nature encourages stakeholders to share critical intelligence, encouraging a proactive approach to emerging threats.

The effectiveness of these platforms in facilitating timely threat intelligence exchange is fundamentally tied to their operational frameworks and community engagement. By standardizing the method of information exchange, these platforms enable organizations to quickly disseminate knowledge regarding new vulnerabilities or threat scenarios. For instance, platforms that utilize machine learning algorithms can analyze large datasets from connected devices and identify patterns that suggest possible security incidents. This real-time analysis provides organizations with actionable insights, allowing them to respond swiftly to mitigate risks before they escalate. Furthermore, integrating automated notifications within these platforms ensures that crucial information reaches stakeholders in a timely manner, thus maintaining robust security postures amid a rapidly evolving threat landscape. Regular participation in these shared environments often correlates with increased resilience, as organizations benefit from collective intelligence that transcends individual capabilities.

To optimize the utilization of these platforms, cyber security professionals should focus on fostering collaboration and maintaining active participation within the information-sharing community. Engaging in forums, contributing to shared databases, and utilizing standardized protocols for communication can enhance the overall security landscape. Establishing clear policies for the exchange of information will not only augment organizational defences but also support a culture of transparency and cooperation in the fight against IoT-related threats. Such proactive measures can significantly elevate the protection of sensitive data and systems as interconnected devices continue to proliferate.

13.3 Building Trust in Information Sharing Networks

Trust is a foundational element in establishing effective information sharing networks, especially in the context of cybersecurity. When organizations and individuals trust one another, they are more willing to share critical data, insights, and intelligence that can significantly enhance overall security posture. In environments where devices like IoT are proliferating, the stakes are higher. Vulnerabilities in one device can compromise entire networks, making trust essential for collaborative risk management. Trust reduces hesitation to report incidents or share threat intelligence, enabling quicker responses to emerging threats. Without a solid foundation of trust, communication can break down, leading to siloed information and ultimately, greater vulnerabilities across the security landscape.

Fostering trust among participants in shared security initiatives requires intentional strategies. Establishing clear communication channels is vital; these channels ensure that all parties understand the expectations and responsibilities in sharing information. Training and education play a crucial role in creating a culture of trust, where participants feel confident about the data they share and the platforms used for communication. Furthermore, implementing robust security measures, such as encryption and access controls, not only protects shared information but also demonstrates a commitment to safeguarding participant contributions. Regularly engaging in trust-building activities, such as workshops or collaborative projects, can reinforce relationships and encourage open dialogue. Finally, recognizing and rewarding contributions from participants can help build a positive framework where trust thrives, making the network more resilient against cyber threats.

In the realm of information sharing networks, trust is not static; it needs continuous nurturing. Cybersecurity professionals should actively seek to cultivate an environment where trust can grow, leading to more effective collaboration. Being transparent about processes, sharing both successes and failures, and maintaining consistent communication can solidify trust among stakeholders. By prioritizing these elements, organizations can build stronger networks that improve their security posture and enhance collective resilience against evolving threats. Consider establishing regular trust audits or feedback loops to gauge the trust level within the network, allowing for timely adjustments and improved partnership dynamics.

14. Challenges and Barriers to IoT Security

14.1 Technical Challenges in Securing IoT

The proliferation of Internet of Things (IoT) devices has created a dynamic ecosystem with diverse functionalities, yet this complexity brings with it a myriad of technical challenges in securing these devices. Many IoT devices are inherently limited in processing power and memory, which restricts the implementation of sophisticated security protocols. These constraints mean that manufacturers often prioritize functionality over security in the design phase, leading to vulnerabilities across the ecosystem. Additionally, the vast variety of devices—from smart home appliances to industrial sensors—introduces inconsistency in security standards, as different manufacturers may employ varying levels of security measures. Communication between these devices across different networks also adds a layer of risk, especially when data is transmitted without proper encryption. Moreover, the rapid pace of deployment often outstrips the ability to monitor and manage security risks effectively, leaving systems open to attacks.

These technical issues significantly impede organizations' efforts to secure their networks. The lack of standardized security protocols means organizations often struggle to implement consistent security measures across all devices. Patching vulnerabilities in IoT devices can also be labour-intensive and complicated, especially if devices are spread out across locations or if their users are not easily reachable. This often results in security gaps that malicious actors can exploit. Furthermore, the interconnected nature of IoT ecosystems means that a breach in one device can potentially compromise a broader network, cascading the impact throughout an organization. Organizations may also find it challenging to identify and respond to security threats in real-time due to the sheer volume of data generated by IoT devices, which can overwhelm existing security monitoring systems. This underscores the urgent need for comprehensive security strategies tailored specifically for IoT environments.

To navigate these challenges effectively, security professionals must adopt a proactive approach to IoT security. Leveraging principles such as segmentation, where IoT devices are isolated within separate networks, can mitigate the risks of a widespread breach. Regular updates and a commitment to maintaining device security hygiene are equally critical. As IoT continues to evolve, staying informed about emerging threats and advancements in security technologies will equip organizations to better protect their networks and adapt to the unique challenges posed by this rapidly expanding landscape.

14.2 Economic and Resource Constraints

The adoption of IoT technologies in various sectors has accelerated, driven by the promise of enhanced efficiency and connectivity. However, the economic and resource constraints significantly impede the implementation of robust IoT security initiatives. Many organizations, particularly smaller entities, struggle with limited budgets and resources, making it challenging to invest in advanced security solutions tailored for IoT environments. The costs associated with deploying comprehensive security measures, such as advanced firewalls, intrusion detection systems, and continuous monitoring tools, can be prohibitive. Furthermore, the ongoing expenses related to maintaining and updating these systems can stretch finances even further. This creates a scenario where organizations may prioritize operational costs over security, leaving them vulnerable to potential breaches.

To address these challenges, smaller organizations can explore several cost-effective solutions that enhance their IoT security posture without requiring significant financial investment. Utilizing open-source security tools can be an effective way to implement security measures while conserving budgets. Engaging in comprehensive employee training and awareness programs about IoT security risks can also yield substantial benefits without incurring high costs. Additionally, leveraging cloud-based security services can provide scalable solutions that adjust according to an organization's need and budget. Such platforms often offer strong security features at a fraction of the cost of on-premises solutions. By adopting a strategic approach to security that emphasizes risk management and prioritizes critical assets, smaller organizations can better safeguard their IoT environments and effectively mitigate potential threats.

Organizations should also consider forming collaborative partnerships with industry peers to share resources and insights on security best practices. This not only spreads the financial burden but also fosters a community of learning and adaptation that can enhance overall security effectiveness. By focusing on these approaches, organizations can work towards building a resilient cybersecurity framework that effectively addresses the unique challenges posed by the IoT landscape.

14.3 Cultural Barriers to Security Implementation

Cultural factors deeply influence how security measures are implemented within organizations. An organization's culture can either support or hinder the acceptance and adherence to security policies. Different teams may have varying levels of awareness about cyber threats, which can lead to an inconsistent approach to security. For instance, an IT department may prioritize robust security protocols, while marketing teams might be more concerned about user experience, potentially neglecting critical security measures. Furthermore, cultural attitudes towards authority and compliance can further complicate implementation; employees in cultures with low power distance may challenge top-down directives, while those in high-context cultures might resist transparency regarding security incidents. Recognizing these cultural dimensions is essential for effective communication and interaction when implementing security protocols across diverse teams.

Overcoming resistance to security measures requires a multi-faceted approach that considers these cultural nuances. Engaging employees by fostering a culture of security awareness is vital. Training sessions that emphasize the importance of security in everyday tasks can help demystify security protocols and illustrate their direct relevance to employees' roles. Additionally, involving team members in the development of security strategies can create a sense of ownership and reduce feelings of imposed measures. Practical initiatives, such as security champions within each department, can serve as liaisons, translating complex security concepts into relatable practices. Furthermore, recognizing and rewarding compliant behaviours can reinforce positive actions towards adherence. By addressing the cultural barriers and facilitating dialogue, organizations can build a more security-conscious workforce.

Providing ongoing support and communication can significantly enhance the culture surrounding security practices. Regular updates on the organization's security posture and sharing success stories can motivate employees to engage with security measures proactively. Additionally, tailoring communication based on the specific needs of teams may further bridge the gap between security intent and actual practice. Consider implementing feedback loops to understand employee sentiments and areas of concern, allowing for continuous improvement in security policies. By being attentive to cultural dynamics and responsive to the workforce's needs, security professionals can ensure smoother implementation of security measures across the organization.

15. Conclusion: The Road Ahead for IoT and Cyber Security

15.1 Summary of Key Takeaways

The preceding chapters have delved into the complex landscape of the Internet of Things (IoT) and its significant implications for the field of cyber security. One of the most crucial insights is the exponential growth of connected devices, which has rapidly expanded the attack surface for potential cyber threats. Security professionals must recognize that traditional security measures may not be sufficient in this new environment. It is essential to adopt a proactive approach, emphasizing the importance of robust security protocols, regular updates, and thorough risk assessments to protect the integrity of networks and sensitive data. Furthermore, the necessity for collaboration among IT, operational technology, and security teams has been underscored. This multidisciplinary approach ensures comprehensive security strategies that account for the unique risks associated with IoT devices.

Another significant aspect highlighted throughout the chapters is the intricate relationship between IoT and cyber security. As IoT devices become increasingly integrated into various sectors, from healthcare to smart cities, the vulnerabilities these devices introduce cannot be overlooked. Cyber security must evolve in tandem with IoT technology, addressing the specific challenges posed by the integration of these devices into existing networks. Security professionals are urged to focus not only on defending networks against external threats but also on understanding the security features of IoT devices themselves. Ensuring that devices are designed with security in mind is crucial. Implementing best practices such as secure coding, authentication measures, and regular security audits can significantly mitigate risks.

In the ever-evolving landscape of IoT and its implications for network security, professionals must remain vigilant and adaptable. Embracing a mindset of continuous learning and staying informed about the latest developments in technology and threats is vital. Building strong security foundations today allows organizations to better safeguard their networks against the innovative attacks of tomorrow. As a practical tip, cybersecurity teams should invest in specialized training focusing on IoT security vulnerabilities and mitigation strategies. This not only boosts individual expertise but also strengthens the organization's overall resilience against cyber threats.

15.2 Strategic Recommendations for Cyber Security Professionals

Cybersecurity professionals engaged with Internet of Things (IoT) devices need to adopt a multi-faceted approach to secure these increasingly ubiquitous technologies. It's essential to incorporate strong encryption on all IoT communication channels and ensure secure firmware updates are a standard part of the device lifecycle. Regularly auditing and updating default passwords used by these devices can significantly enhance security. Additionally, implementing network segmentation helps isolate IoT devices from critical company assets, thus limiting potential exposure during a breach. Consistent monitoring of device behaviour for unusual activity can further aid in early detection of security incidents, enabling prompt response and mitigation.

Adopting a proactive and adaptive approach to IoT security practices is crucial in today's fast-evolving technological landscape. Cybersecurity professionals should prioritize continuous education and awareness, staying informed about emerging threats and vulnerabilities in IoT devices. This includes regularly participating in training sessions and threat intelligence sharing forums, which can help in developing a more robust security posture. Moreover, integrating adaptive security measures that learn and evolve with new threats can greatly enhance resilience. Utilizing artificial intelligence and machine learning to analyze patterns and predict potential breaches allows for speedier and more effective responses to incidents.

In the realm of IoT security, collaboration among teams is key. Encouraging an interdisciplinary approach that involves IT departments, operations, and even third-party vendors can lead to a more comprehensive security strategy. Additionally, always consider legal and compliance aspects related to data protection and user privacy, as these can impact the overall security framework. Keeping abreast of regulatory changes and adapting security measures accordingly can help mitigate legal risks. Ultimately, creating a culture of security awareness within the organization ensures that every team member understands their role in safeguarding IoT devices and contributes to a unified defense mechanism.

15.3 Preparing for the Future of IoT Security

As the Internet of Things (IoT) expands, it brings both incredible opportunities and significant security challenges. Staying ahead of evolving threats and rapid technology changes requires a proactive approach. One effective strategy is to adopt a layered security framework, which means implementing multiple levels of security measures that address different kinds of vulnerabilities. These layers could include robust encryption protocols for data transmission, secure device onboarding processes, and regular security audits to ensure compliance with the latest regulations and best practices. Additionally, fostering strong partnerships with device manufacturers and service providers can lead to shared knowledge and a more unified approach to security across the IoT ecosystem. Engaging in threat intelligence sharing with industry peers further enhances this strategy by enabling organizations to stay informed about emerging threats and vulnerabilities.

The importance of continuous learning and adaptation in cybersecurity cannot be overstated, especially in the context of IoT. The landscape is constantly changing, requiring cybersecurity professionals to stay engaged with ongoing education and training opportunities. Participating in workshops, webinars, and online courses can help professionals keep their skills sharp and updated. Engaging with cybersecurity communities, forums, and social media platforms allows professionals to share insights and learn from real-world experiences. Additionally, organizations should cultivate a culture of learning, encouraging teams to experiment with new tools and technologies, which can foster innovation and agility in addressing security challenges.

To effectively prepare for the future of IoT security, it's crucial to implement a mindset geared towards adaptability. As new technologies emerge, staying informed about their implications on security can lead to timely adjustments in strategies and policies. Regularly reassessing security posture and integrating the latest advancements in threat detection and response technology will ensure a robust defense against potential attacks. Always remember that proactive preparation and an ethos of learning are key elements in navigating the complexities of IoT security.